Walking With You
for Grieving Grandparents

Published by:
Sufficient Grace Ministries for Women, Inc.
P.O. Box 243
Deshler, Ohio 43516

This book is a combination of writings from Kelly Gerken and a compilation of stories from grieving grandparents around the world.

Edited and formatted by: Adrienne Freytag
Cover Image: Tienne Wilkin
Cover Design: Bethany Conkel, Maria Elkins

ISBN-13: 978-1986730013
ISBN-10: 1986730018

Dedication

Special thanks to the SGM team and the brave and beautiful grandparents who have contributed thoughts from the most sacred places of their hearts to complete this book. It is our privilege to walk this path with so many amazing families. We remember each of your precious grandchildren with you. Thank you for offering the wisdom you have gleaned, in hopes that other mothers and fathers will know they do not walk alone.

Rejoice with those who rejoice,
and weep with those who weep.

~ Romans 12:15 ~

Table of Contents

If You Have Just Heard or If You Are Currently at the Hospital............1

Include Grandparents..2

Grandparents, We See You 5

Stories From the Hearts of Grieving Grandparents.....................6

The Hardest Thing..21

Regrets..25

Wrestling With Faith..28

When You Can't Pray..29

Understanding Perspective – Communication between Parents and
Grandparents..32

What Bereaved Parents Wish Grandparents Understood About
Providing Support Through Grief...35

Remembering & Including Your Grandchild in Family Traditions........47

Helpful Ways to Offer Comfort and Support to Grieving Grandparents
....48

Be Sensitive to a Grandparent's Compounded Grief Story 48

What Grieving Grandparents Wish Friends, Family, and
Caregivers Understood 54

From One Grandparent's Heart to Another 64

Allow Yourself Time to Grieve..67

Be Gentle With Yourself as You Grieve.....................................69

Helpful Resources 72

Online Support for Grieving Grandparents 72

Books for Grieving Grandparents..72

Memory-Making and Support...72

If You Have Just Heard or If You Are Currently at the Hospital

Dear Grandparent,

If you are reading this book, you have most likely heard the devastating words that changed your life and the life of your family forever. Babies aren't supposed to die. It goes against everything in the natural order of life. When it happens, it shakes the foundation of the entire family. I'm so sorry for the loss of your precious grandchild. As a grandparent, you carry not only the pain of your own grief, but the grief of your child and their partner. While so much is lost in that tragic moment, there are still some things that can bring some comfort to you and your family as you welcome this baby earthside. This little one is worth remembering, worth celebrating.

While some suggestions may feel difficult to consider in the midst of shock, grief, and a myriad of other emotions, many families find some healing in creating tangible memories with their grandbaby. Grandparents are often looking for a way to help their child find comfort and hope in the midst of this pain. Spending time making memories and getting photos of baby can bring some of that comfort and hope to a painful time. Joy can even be woven in the midst of the brokenness.

Include Grandparents

Feeling helpless as your own child is hurting and grieving is crippling. If you are a parent, caregiver, support person, or even a family member reading this, include the grandparents. Include them in the care of the baby if you are in the room with the family. The baby's mother is sometimes not feeling well or up for all the baby care…bathing and dressing of baby immediately after she gives birth. (Although if she is, please allow her and baby's father to do this! Always offer parents the opportunity and give them the options to decide about baby care.) If the parents are open to it, include the grandparents in this healing time of memory-making. Parents can still bathe baby, if they would like, and grandparents can help in another way. Perhaps applying lotion to the baby after parents bathe. When parents and grandparents are offered options and given the opportunity, baby care and memory-making will naturally and beautifully flow together.

If you are the grandparent reading, please understand if parents don't know how to include you in this time. They have never done this before, and their own pain is bigger than anything else. They may react with so many different emotions, and because you are their safe person, you will likely see them all. Find ways to gently stay involved…ways to help them that they may not know they need, while also respecting the space of your grieving children if that's what they require. Perhaps making a blanket, buying or making an outfit, offering to make phone calls or help with funeral arrangements, sending over some homemade meals or gift cards to restaurants they like for when they are feeling up to going out, and offering to watch their other children are all ways you can provide tangible support to the parents.

As time goes by, know that it will mean so much to the child's parents if you continue to find ways to honor and include the memory of your grandchild in family celebrations and when you are doing things for your living grandchildren. It is typically a comfort if you remember with them.

Even if a baby's life has been brief, there are ways to honor your grandchild's memory.

- Have a teddy bear to hold for comfort.
- Keep a tiny bear or a keepsake close to the size of your grandchild.
- Keep an ultrasound picture - Ask for one if it is not offered.
- Use your grandchild's name.
- Wrap your grandchild in a special blanket. Wraps are available, even for very tiny babies. You can also request a keepsake wrap if you do not meet your grandchild in person.
- Play a special song.
- Journal your thoughts, dreams, and feelings.
- Write letters to your grandchild.
- Take photos, even of tiny babies.
- Pray together.
- Bring special jewelry or other items that you would like with you and/or your grandchild in a photograph.
- Read a book to your grandchild.
- Complete a special memory book.
- If the baby is not too fragile, take time to bathe and dress your grandchild.
- Spend time saying hello and goodbye.
- Keep your grandchild with you as long as you would like.
- Perform a Baptism, Dedication, Naming Ceremony or other ceremonies that are important to you and your family.

Arrangements should be made to have professional photographers available. Sufficient Grace Ministries is an organization who not only provides professional photography, but also offer perinatal hospice support as part of an array of their services and support, all free of charge. There are other organizations, such as Now I Lay Me Down to Sleep, who also provide photography services for families facing the loss of a baby.

Do not allow others to determine how you spend this time. This is your opportunity to fill a lifetime of memories into moments. Spend it the way you see fit. Respect and encourage the way parents wish to spend that time creating memories, even if you do not understand or agree with all their choices. And, don't rush or allow others to rush you.

Grandparents, We See You

When a baby dies, it is not just the parent who experiences the impact of loss and grief. The entire family and friends of the parents feel the weight of sorrow. Siblings, aunts, uncles, cousins, grandparents, and friends all feel the effects of the loss of the baby and the deep desire to find ways to support the grieving parents, even as their own hearts are broken.

I stand at the hospital bed of many of those families as a perinatal loss comfort companion (comfort doula). Time and time again, I see the devastation in the eyes of the grandparents, as they feel broken that their grandchild has died and helpless in the face of their child's pain.

"What do we do?" grandparents will ask with agony in their eyes.

There's a strong desire for grandparents to protect their children, to fix this broken, to make the pain better. Only, we all know there's nothing that can heal this wound in a moment's time. There's no kissing away this "boo-boo," no band-aid big enough to cover the oozing.

"I'm so sorry," I will often whisper, "This is a double dose for you as a grandparent. You have your own grief for your grandbaby. But, also, that's your baby (referring to the mom in the hospital bed or the bewildered father in the corner). She is in the worst pain of her life. And, you can't make this better...you can't protect her from this pain."

As in most support situations, recognizing and validating a person's struggle or pain helps to give it a name. It also gives us understanding for our own helpless feelings, to know that what we

5

are experiencing is a common response under the circumstances, and it helps us to know that we are not alone. Someone sees us. We need support, too.

Grandparents were planning, waiting, and dreaming for this precious baby right along with the child's parents. They are not only part of the story, but they have their own stories to tell. Stories of much wanted and longed for babies. Stories filled with plans and dreams that were changed forever with the words, "I'm so sorry... there is no heartbeat."

Their stories are worth telling, and the pain they feel is worth acknowledging. Every story, just like every single baby represented holds precious value. Their words resonate with the hearts of other grandparents who are missing their grandchildren while trying to support their own broken-hearted children.

Stories From the Hearts of Grieving Grandparents

Carla -

I still remember getting a phone call late one night and my daughter saying "Momma, we lost the baby." I can't think about that moment without tearing up and feeling the pain squeezing my heart and it has been many years ago.

My daughter had to deliver normally. Her sister and I were by her side with her husband. The doctor told us that we could hold the baby if we choose to. I knew that if I didn't, I would not be able to deal with the tremendous hole in my heart. Holding her and just looking at her angelic face and simply whispering how much she was loved and wanted gave me some peace.

Charlene -

Callen taught us more about love in 30 short days then I knew in my 64 years on this earth. (Born at 26 weeks, he lived for 30 precious days.)

Kathy T. -

Our grandchild already had a name before his Mommy delivered him. My grandson's name was Xander. His Papal and myself already made big plans for Xander... singing Little Bunny Foo Foo, reading him one of many Dr. Seuss's books, getting dirty

6

playing with some Tonka trucks, buying him his first baseball bat, and spoiling him rotten. My fondest memory was rocking my grandson, Xander, following his stillbirth in the delivery room.

We were very involved with providing support and comfort to Xander's parents before and after delivery. At moments feeling helpless for your daughter and son-in-law wanting so much to take their pain away or say the right thing at the right moment to comfort them. Sometimes the silence in the delivery room spoke louder than any words uttered... the silent prayers and the love in the room were tangible and heartfelt.

The staff gave the family all the time needed to hold baby Xander and I treasured the opportunity to give him some Gigi loving.

Papal Tim -
Xander was stillborn at 26 weeks. Safe in the arms of God, Xander was called home to receive his Angel wings. GG and Papal had high aspirations, dreams, and plans for our third born Grandson. Plans of teaching you how to fish, climbing the apple tree, riding your first bike, playing in the dirt with Tonka trucks, sitting on the back porch on a hot summer night eating popsicles... watching the fireflies dancing about the treetops as if they were blinking lights on our Christmas tree, taking you for a ride on the tractor as we did with your cousin. We would stand in awe at the wonder and amazement in your eyes.

Karen -
The experience of being at the birth of my stillborn granddaughter was an indescribable moment. Her hair was golden, and I held her and told her about her amazing mother. I will always cherish this moment. I carry the photo in my phone. It is my keepsake.

Mary -
My husband and I cried and clung to each other, then quickly packed and made the 6 1/2-hour drive to be with our son and his wife. I made calls along the drive to let family and close friends

know. I was so worried she would deliver before we got there. All the hopes and dreams I had for this little boy kept running through my mind...

I will never forget our son coming out to the waiting room and bursting into tears saying, "he is so beautiful." We all hugged and cried. The balloons in the gift shop announcing, "It's a boy!" were impossible to look at. Every time a baby was born, a lullaby was played over the loudspeaker. Our baby did not have a lullaby played for him. We all had turns holding him, telling little Oliver whatever was in our hearts. Our son took pictures that I haven't looked at since but will someday.

I have no regrets about the time we spent together and with him. I think as hard as it was, it was important that we held him and had that time together, two families together to support each other.

Every time a baby was born,
a lullaby was played over the loudspeaker...
Our baby did not have a lullaby played for him.

Mary - Oliver's Grandmother

Anita -
Our grandson, Cayden, came into this world on October 21, the day before my birthday and 3 days before his grandpa's birthday. He was beautiful, healthy, strong and so smart! We had the opportunity to have him and his parents live with us for 4 months, so we got the blessings of being able to bond and help with daily care.

I have so many precious memories of him, but the one that stands out is when he was tired or fussy and I would take him and wrap him in my arms and feel his little body just melt into me. He would instantly be calm as I whispered in his ear and kissed his cheek and walked as I sang or hummed, you are my sunshine, my only sunshine. He was right over my heart, and it was like our hearts melded together in those times.

8

Cayden just didn't wake up the morning of June 9th. He was 7 1/2 months old.

Michael -

Our third grandchild, Oliver Martin Gensler (Yes, OMG), died the day before he was due to be born.

That was 23 days 4 months and 5 years ago, and his death is still the most horrible thing that ever happened to me and my family. In fact, from that point in time forward, every time someone in our family begins to walk through a difficult time (my loss of a job at 60 years old, our daughter's divorce, the death of my wife's father...) we now begin such painful journeys with the awareness that we've already walked through the most horrible experience ever, we can walk through this too. That said, Oliver is still our most beloved third grandchild and we will never ever forget him. Rachel and Daniel walked through this unimaginable tragedy with a courage and resiliency that is beyond anyone's years. My wife and I, along with Daniel's parents, walked uncomfortably in Rachel and Daniel's footsteps because none of us had ever had to live through the death of our child.

We were faced with not knowing what to say or what to do as two of our children faced a tragedy beyond our experience or expertise. But, we did it together, though mounds of tears and grief, through massive imposing doors of impossibility, one massive door at a time. Rachel and Daniel leading the way. Grandparents, brothers and sisters, family and friends following in their footsteps.

As a family, we surrounded Rachel and Daniel for the next hours, days, and weeks -- but we were always steps behind them in this journey. We had no certain words of advice because we had no comparable experience. All we had was love and our own first time raw experience of grief. And we watched in utter awe at how Rachel and Daniel walked their path ahead of us: deciding on induced labor for Oliver's birth (rather than a C-section because of various risks but mainly its impact on future pregnancies and births), sitting though the hours and hours of waiting for our dead grandson's birth, most of that time in the room with Rachel and Daniel, but at the end from outside in the waiting room, leaving

Daniel and Rachel alone with the doctor to bring their first child into their waiting arms only after his death.

They then spent some alone time with their first born before sending word that their family could now come join them to welcome Oliver into our family.

Nancy and I went first to Rachel, our baby girl. Then we turned our attention and hearts and arms to our grandson Oliver. Everyone took turns holding little Oliver.

Tonya -
The greatest memory was and is watching the walk of love. Knowing that the short-lived life of Saylor Grace made a big impact on others. The precious memories etched in my heart of her sweet face and smile, her tiny feet and fingers.

His death is still the most horrible thing

that ever happened to me and my family.

In fact, from that point in time forward,

whenever someone in our family begins

to walk through a difficult time

(my loss of a job at 60 years old,

our daughter's divorce, the death of my wife's father...)

we now begin such painful journeys

with the awareness that we've already walked

through the most horrible experience ever,

we can walk through this too.

Michael – Oliver's Grandfather

Patty -

Our beautiful granddaughter Gianna Marie was born with Trisomy 18. We held her in our arms and knew she wouldn't be with us long but all we saw was the miracle of her birth and the blessing she gave us. We believe we witnessed one of God's miracles. She wasn't breathing when she was born, and the priest baptized her immediately and she began breathing. The hardest thing was watching her suffer as she was preparing to be in God's arms.

We were there for the whole process and thank our children for including us. There is not much to say during this time. You watch your children suffer and in pain and you just pray.

Our granddaughter lived for 48 hours. We were there when she passed along with her other grandparents. We gave each other support while our children and grandchildren grieved.

Sharla -

At about 7 months gestational age our precious Lily's heart stopped beating.

Although we were at the hospital with our daughter, I wasn't involved with Lily's birth/delivery. The nurses and then the doctor would not let us in to see our daughter once the ultrasound showed no heartbeat. We were devastated when the doctor finally told me that Lily, as he put it "did not make it." I regret not being with my daughter to help comfort and hold her right after Lily's birth... my heart was breaking because I couldn't be with my daughter.

Being there at the hospital, waiting to see our daughter, then finally being in the room with her gave my heart some relief. To see my daughter and hold her helped me to some degree.

Sarah -

My husband and I were blessed to be with our daughter throughout her entire labor and delivery. I was there to hold her hand and witness the birth. I was so happy I could be there, and I have no regrets.

11

Joi -

I was caring for Ezekiel's 3-year-old sister, Eden, at her home in Taiwan during his birth. She and I excitedly traveled to the hospital to greet her new brother on his birthday and spent the evening in the hospital loving on him with Eden asking dozens of questions!

Thirteen days later I was again caring for Eden at her home when Ezekiel died. Eden was having trouble sleeping, worried about her brother's surgery, so she and I were making a "tent" on top of the bed, planning to climb inside and read books by flashlight, when my daughter called with the news that 13 day old Ezekiel had died. I instinctively screamed out a gut-wrenching "NO!!!!!" until I saw the panic on Eden's face and did my best to contain my sudden, overwhelming unbelief and desperation.

My daughter told me someone from their church was coming to pick up Eden and I go to the hospital --- and would I please pick out clothes for Ezekiel to wear to the hospital morgue, all he had worn had been hospital gowns.

Unbeknownst to me, my daughter asked a friend, who is a photographer, to come to the hospital and take photographs of the time immediately after Ezekiel's death.

In Taiwan they have a practice of the family washing the deceased person's body and dressing them to go to the morgue (most persons are cremated in Taiwan due to limited land availability). I stood in the PICU room where I had spent most of my limited time with my new grandson and watched my daughter and her husband bathe and dress their sweet 2-week-old baby for the first time.

Eden happily held her baby brother for the first time in almost two weeks, not fully understanding that he had just crossed over to life eternal. Family friends put ink on Ezekiel's little hands and feet and made his prints. His little body was loved on by anyone present who desired to hold him. Initially reluctant to hold him, fearing I couldn't handle it, I finally held my lifeless grandson's body and marveled at his beauty. All the wires and tubes were gone, his little CPAP was missing, and no surgical masks were required

12

to care for him. I was finally able to kiss his sweet cheeks unhindered.

At first, I was reluctant to participate in the photographs of Ezekiel after death. I guess my old- fashioned thinking of photographing the dead as morbid interfered. But I soon was lost in the precious looks of love and the care my daughter, her husband, and Eden had for Ezekiel, and in the realization of the glory of the moment -- that my precious grandson was now in the presence of my Savior!!

Those gathered in that room that night were believers and we began singing hymns and praises. My heart and mind were a mixture of overwhelming grief and loss, yet trying to grasp Ezekiel's death from God's perspective. A lot of that night is a blur in my memory.

Since I was so far away from my home, my husband, my church and even my country, I felt very alone in my grief. In the days that followed, I remember feeling like everything I said was the wrong thing and would cause more tears and pain for my daughter. Thankfully my daughter and her husband had many friends and church family to support and care for them. And God provided for my other daughter and my son to travel to Taiwan to be present for Ezekiel's memorial service and to help share our burden of grief.

The year anniversary of Ezekiel's death occurred about a month ago and for the first time I looked closely at the pictures from the night of his death. I'm so thankful we have those pictures! It breaks my heart that we have more pictures of him dead than alive, but I can see now that that night was a very sacred night, and the pictures don't seem morbid to me anymore.

Debbie -

I will never forget that phone call. It was a beautiful sunny day and I was outside playing with my stepdaughter's 2 children, enjoying life. My daughter-in-love called to tell me that they had lost our precious baby. She and I talked and cried together. My heart was breaking for my loss but the heartbreak my son and his wife were going through was unimaginable.

13

My son has kept his emotions in about the loss and doesn't talk about it with anyone but his wife, so I have been unable to share his grief other than to let him know how very much I love him. In memory of my precious grandson, I got a tattoo with his name so that he will always be remembered. Last year at our family reunion, we released a balloon with his name on it as well as the message, 'I will hold you in my heart until I can hold you in my arms'.

Nancy -

My daughter carried Claire to term. One day her heart stopped beating before Kim went into labor. An ultrasound confirmed that Claire was dead. I watched them leave for the hospital but then had to go upstairs & act normal for my 3 yr old grandson. There was no one else to care for him. I never got to see or hold Claire.

I was there to care for my grandson. I wish I had been able to see/hold Claire, but I know my being there for Ian made things easier for my kids. They didn't have to worry about Ian. They could concentrate on the decisions involved with inducing Claire.

Sonya -

September 14th, 2014. We lost our grandson John Luke Odom. He was stillborn. We knew that he was gone the day before and my son and daughter-in-law prepared for him to enter the world silently. He was tiny and beautiful. We all had time to spend saying goodbye.

We were all in the delivery room. It was a beautiful and breathtaking experience. It is hard to know what to say and do. What I found out is it is best to say nothing. Be quiet and just be there.

The pain of that loss and watching our youngest son hold his son was almost unbearable but through the Grace of our Almighty God we have seen it through. After their loss my son and daughter-in-law raised money through different fundraisers and donations to donate a Cuddle Cot to the hospital where Luke was born. God has opened doors and our eyes, experiencing His Love through a tiny silent baby boy named John Luke Odom.

Cathy -
Our grandbabies were born early at 20-21 weeks gestation. My husband and I had the opportunity to hold and kiss our babies prior to their passing away. I was with my daughter and her husband as the babies were born.

Susie -
My grief encircles more than one grandchild. I don't know if grief is compounded by numbers and with time, but I am deeply heartbroken for my three daughters, their families, and those aching arms of theirs and ours. Seven grandbabies in heaven, three were babies old enough to hold, without breath - but only for a tiny time, trying to see and take in each little finger and toe, their precious faces... and then seeing them in caskets, and later watching as the dirt filled up their graves after a funeral. The other four were miscarriages and a tubal pregnancy.

Rick -
We were there. The experience was and remains a nightmare. I remember God sending us one incredible nurse after another. I remember seeing and hearing all over again what remarkable parents Amanda and Nick are.

We were well supported at the hospital and through our church. Words cannot express how loving people have been in both of those places.

Dave and Mary Jo -
It was discovered at 12 weeks gestation that our grandson had an anomaly condition PUV that would give him a fatal diagnosis. We walked with complete faith with our daughter and son-in-law through the pregnancy praying for a miracle.

Our little grandson, Samuel, was born at 35 weeks gestation and breathing and looking perfect (not at all what the doctors had predicted). We got to spend a brief amount of time with him before they took him to a hospital that had the ability to care for him in a NICU unit because he was doing so well.

He passed away 4 hours after his birth. He was beautiful and looked so much like his father with a little of his mother for good measure. :-) It was a very Holy moment with him. So many of the hospital staff was present after his birth and stood in amazement. We felt like we were surrounded with a crowd of witnesses to these precious moments. Because he was delivered by C-section our daughter was in the delivery room being stitched up and she missed these moments. They finally brought her in before he left, but she only got to hold his hand and caress his hair. She never got to hold him alive.

His daddy, two uncles, and I (grandpa) went with him to the other hospital. When it became evident that he would not survive his daddy told him he was going to go be with Jesus and he and his mommy loved him very much. I (grandma) stayed with our daughter at the hospital where he was delivered.

Sarah B. -
Ryeder was born with the expectations to die- and that's just how the doctors reminded us every appointment. He blessed us with his presence for almost 8 months. He was the most comforting thing in my life and losing him has been the most challenging thing I've ever had to go through. The hardest thing to do was look at my first born and see all the pain in her eyes as she held her first born dead in her arms and hearing her say "mom why". Ryeder has definitely left his mark in our lives and no day is ever easy. Every day I feel like I'm dragging. There are still things that make me cry.

I've been fully involved in his birth and death. I stayed by my daughter's side through both events. I gave him CPR. The night before he passed, I was supposed to babysit him. She and I had an argument. So, I made her take him home. I wish I would have kept him, just to have had another night with him. We made molds of his hands and feet, took his handprint and footprint, and even prints of his lips. We cut his hair, we even spent alone time with him at the funeral home.

16

Grandparent -

There was nothing we could do or say, all we could do was be there and keep our granddaughter safe. Dreadful, we felt so helpless. Thankfully we were encouraged by the midwives and by our daughter and son-in-law to spend some time with our grandson, to hold him and bond with him. We took some photos and they are very much treasured now.

To be honest, we didn't feel supported at all... we were given a SANDS leaflet by our daughter's midwife and I suppose that was of some practical use. Some of our friends allowed us to talk freely and show them pictures of our grandson and that helped. I read as many books and articles as I could get my hands on. It is shocking to find out just how many babies are stillborn every day in the UK and yet you feel so alone when it happens to your family.

Lorrie -

I lost my granddaughter, Ruthie Lou, six years ago. She has taught me so much about love and life, about spiritual and earthly connections, and about grieving. I remember sitting in a rocking chair in the NICU and holding her. I was focusing on rocking and comforting her, and after a while, I realized she was the one comforting me. I felt like I was floating on a cloud as I held her in my arms. I miss her so much.

Our granddaughter was born with chromosomal abnormalities and lived for 33 very precious days after her birth.

Maria -

Amalya had anencephaly. He was born at 37 weeks 2 days, and he lived one hour and twenty minutes.

Amalya was delivered via C-section to maximize the potential for him to be born alive. Six grandparents, three great-grandparents, and multiple aunts and uncles were all present at the hospital. Amalya's parents were very generous with their limited time with their first-born son. Each grandparent had the opportunity to hold precious Amalya before he passed away.

We loved the memory-making time. I have Amalya's handprints and footprints in my Bible, which is a treasured tradition we have continued with our other grandchildren.

Brenda -

Rylee was our first grandchild. She was due July 22, 2010. On March 16, 2010 (our 25th wedding anniversary) we found out she was a girl. We were so excited and could not wait to meet and hold her.

At my daughter's 38-week checkup she was told there was no heartbeat. She was induced that night and delivered Rylee shortly after 4 a.m. Rylee had umbilical cord torsion.

We were in the room with our daughter until it was time for her to push. We left the room for the delivery. I just wish we would have taken more pictures of Rylee. We have some but that's all we have of her.

Janella -

MicKenzie passed away as a result of anencephaly. She was born into this world silently. She was 41 weeks. Yes! We painted her hands and feet to create beautiful artwork. We did clay hand and foot impressions. We will always treasure these very tangible and priceless gifts. We also had a photographer from Now I Lay Me Down to Sleep. We still love looking at every picture. I also was able to make some blankets for her before she was born. Creating her blankets was very healing for me.

Connie -

Our son and daughter in-law came to us one day to announce that they were expecting twins sometime in December. We were so excited and couldn't wait for the babies to arrive. But soon after the news of twins came worry. It was determined that this was a very rare pregnancy and it looked like one of the babies had a birth defect. We soon learned that one of the babies would not survive long after birth. We were heartbroken. I worried for both babies. I worried for my son and daughter in-law. I wanted to take their

18

pain and carry it for them, but I couldn't. We felt so helpless. Our granddaughter Scarlett passed away shortly after birth from a birth defect.

Karen -

We were at the hospital very shortly after he was born. I took lots of pictures and even took a video of him crying. Our son thanked me later for taking the video so that they would always have the sound of their son's cry. The day that they were discharged to go home, we picked up pizza to take to their house for supper. Again, I took lots of pictures. We all held and rocked our new grandson. We were falling very much in love with him. He was so tiny and precious. Later that night, I was awakened by a phone call from our son frantically telling to get to the hospital. Something was wrong with the baby. The nightmare began.

Our grandson passed away when he was 4 days old. Later it was determined that he had a rare metabolic disorder call MCADD. Our son and daughter-in-law were both found by genetic testing to be carriers.

Grandparent -

I carry the loss of my first grandchild secretly in my heart. I can't tell his or her story, because it isn't mine to tell. My son's girlfriend chose to end her pregnancy in the first trimester without telling him about the baby. I share my story here, anonymously, although it is not exactly like the rest, because my grandchild matters. His life matters, even though it was very brief. There are so many layers to the pain I feel as a grandparent who has to carry the knowledge of this sweet baby quietly in my heart, a baby I love even though we've never met...and I didn't have a chance to dream dreams for this precious life. Layers of regret and shame. Layers of pain for my son who did not have a voice or a choice. Layers of longing for what could've been and what has yet to be. I know that my grandbaby is with Jesus, safe in heaven. And, I believe we will meet again one day. I also believe that God will cover us in grace, and I still hope someday to be called Grandma here on earth.

Lisa -

She was born at 24.5 weeks, 15.5 ounces, 11 inches long. Her Mommy had preeclampsia, so they had to deliver Heavenleigh Miracle.

She lived 29 days. She was so sick and so little her body could not handle growing and healing. They took her off everything except the respirator and dressed her in the little micro preemie outfit I bought her. Then she was placed in her mother's arms and they took out the breathing tube.

I was there when the doctor told them they might need to make a decision. They decided no chest compressions if her heart rate were to go low again, only to use medications. Then, after a lot of prayer and tears, the doctor told my son she only had a 10% chance of survival and no word on all the complications she would face. I was there for support every weekend and the day when she was born and the days at the end. I was so proud of my son and daughter-in-law and they were strong, but not strong. The experience was surreal. We all got to hold and rock her for hours and there were special nurses to help with everything. Pictures were taken and molds of keepsakes made.

Pat -
Rosalynn was stillborn. They are not sure why, but she was beautiful.

When I went into the room, my daughter was crying. I held her and didn't know what to say or do... I was numb. What came out of my mouth was "all we have now is hope". Hope that better days are coming. I was at a loss for words... caught up in the unspeakable tragedy.

We were able to baptize Rosalynn. My son in-law used a shell to pour holy water on her. There were several people in the room which was very comforting knowing that friends and family were supporting us in our loss.

The hardest thing...being 100% there for my daughter... I think she was stronger than I was. I feel we are stronger as a family. My daughter started a non-profit organization in Rosalyn's memory by giving bags full of items that we found were very useful while we were in the hospital to mothers going through the same thing. We all helped out in different capacities.

The Hardest Thing

We asked fifty grandparents: What was the hardest thing about the experience of losing your grandchild? The answers overwhelmingly referenced the agony of watching their children grieve the loss of their own baby, while not being able to relieve their pain.

Joi -

As a mom, the most difficult thing I faced was seeing the tremendous grief and pain my daughter was going through and not being able to do anything about it! I felt like I was always saying the wrong thing, bringing more tears, more grief. As a grandmother, the hardest thing was when people implied that since he died so young, he was not to be missed as much --- I struggled with how do you grieve over a baby that you didn't have the privilege to spend much time with --- I have so very, very few memories to dwell on and bring comfort --- I only have unmade memories! There is no word for that --- grief for unmade memories!! Also, a difficult thing has been to process all the regrets that try to creep into my heart and mind --- like why the heck didn't I take off my surgical mask and kiss my sweet grandson on his chubby cheeks when he was in the hospital? Why did I not let my daughter speak of her doubts about Ezekiel's ability to survive surgery? And more regrets that, thankfully, I no longer can recall.

Anonymous -

The hardest thing was to see the despair in my son and daughter-in-law. Mothers are supposed to fix things for their children. This was so hard knowing that I couldn't fix this. The only thing I could do was comfort and be there. I grieved deeply, but privately, in my husband's arms, so that I could be strong for my son and daughter-in-law. I reassured my daughter-in-law that she couldn't have known what was happening. I am sure that the baby died quickly. The umbilical cord twisted and became so thin that nothing could pass through it. My son was so strong for his wife that the nurses commented on how devoted they were to each other. My husband wrote my son a letter telling him what a hero he was for all of us. I was the one to hold my son when he broke down.

Shannon B. -

I was very grateful for the time the hospital gave us to hold and be with Amy. She was born at 3:00 am and we were able to keep her until my daughter was discharged at 10:00 that morning. Then I had to watch my daughter and son-in-law walk out of the room and the hospital with empty arms. It's the hardest thing to watch your child going through this tragedy knowing you cannot take their pain and heartache away and make everything better!

Marcy -

Feeling like I didn't have the right to my grief.... feeling like I couldn't fix it for anyone.... so helpless.... feeling the need, even to this day, to grieve differently than everyone else.

Kristi -

Not being able to make my daughter and son-in-law feel better. Not being able to "fix" things. Feeling helpless. Not knowing who to talk to.

Sarah -

Staying strong for my daughter. Trying to find the answers to her questions. Trying to hold back my tears while she begged for her baby's life. Trying to convince her not to lose her faith.

Anita -
Watching my daughter, trying to hold her and be there for her support but also dying inside.

Rick -
I still have not grieved my own loss as a grandparent. My grief for Amanda, Nick, my wife Carla, and Nick's parents occupies my heart and mind. I don't know when or if I will ever really grieve for myself. My energies are focused on them.

Karen -
The hardest thing was seeing our son and daughter-in-law so devastated with the passing of their newborn baby. They were so very excited for their first child. Having him only 4 days was just not fair. Our son even questioned, "Why God?"

Cindi -
The hardest thing about losing my grandbabies was watching MY baby grieve for HER baby. I'm her mom and I had absolutely no way to take her pain away. It was like a double loss.

Vickie O. -
The grief you feel for the loss of your grandchild is secondary to the grief you feel seeing your child so lost and distraught. Because I knew the love, I also knew the agony, and there's nothing to do but suffer with them.

Susie -
The hardest thing was watching my perfect family become so broken. Yes, I think they all still have their faith, but the whole dynamic of family life is forever changed. I cannot even find words that will express the helplessness a grandparent feels as they watch grief shatter lives in their loved ones. Even our 3-year-old granddaughter play-acts baby deaths - "oh, my baby has died, my baby is dead". That is how life seems to her. Besides the babies in

our family, her daddy's sister also had a baby that died just a few months before her stillborn sister. In her 3 little years she has watched four babies be buried, and recently said the words I feel "all the babies die..." and they do, in our family.

Tracy -
My daughter's grief and for my son-in-law. But watching my daughter grieve, that just about killed me. I just want to take her pain away. I'm so heartbroken that my granddaughter is not here and I'm heartbroken for Malory. Sometimes she will put a picture on Facebook of her and her friends and I will study her face to try and see if she really is doing okay. I feel like her joy of having a baby is forever altered.

Regrets

Regrets are always a part of grief, but even more so after the loss of a child. When a baby dies, there is often little time to find resources or to prepare for memory-making. Most families do not think about what they would do if their baby or grandchild died. In the midst of shock, they are left to navigate through a time filled with great pain and confusion. Families must fit a lifetime of love and memories into moments, often with little support or resources.

A baby's life is so brief, when cut tragically short, there is no way to escape some moments of regret or what-if. We will always long for more time. No matter how prepared we were or how present we were in the moment, it is normal to experience a regret or longing to go back and have one more memory. The truth is, because their lives were taken from us so soon, we may always long for more. As we explore the regrets we wrestle with in our hearts, it's important to remember to give ourselves grace. We did the best we could in the moment, under incredibly painful and tragic circumstances.

Marcy -

My husband and I, along with our other son and daughter, who were young adults at the time, were all in the room when the doctor came in to tell us that they had been unable to save Landon. The grief, shock, despair, and anger that I witnessed is something I have never talked about. I wish I would have taken more pictures.... but I was so afraid of upsetting my daughter.

Kristi -

I was there, at the hospital when the miscarriage happened, and I tried to be there afterwards... but I felt as though she was pushing me away.

Cathy -

The doctors and nurses were empathetic and allowed us to grieve openly. One thing that did bother me was that each little baby was wrapped in a bath towel at birth. Since the birth was unexpected, we had no soft little blankets to wrap them in as we held them. There was no attempt made to save the babies, which I fully understand. They were just too tiny.

Jane C -

I was with my daughter. Biggest regret is not taking photos and him being introduced to his big brothers. No support. Didn't make enough memories.

Dave and Mary Jo -

We were totally involved and present at the delivery - his daddy was with him as he died - I (grandpa) arrived moments later and stayed with him and his daddy for hours after as he was bathed and dressed and they took pictures, made hand molds and foot and hand prints. I stayed with daddy the whole time and drove him back to the hospital to be with Samuel's mommy hours later. I (grandma) was with my daughter (Samuel's mommy). My biggest regret right away is that I did not climb in bed with her right after we received the news that he passed away. I was frozen in my chair - I could not think or speak. She was laying there so beautiful having delivered her first born. We were so excited with the doctor's proclamation that he was doing so well! And then the call came that he died, and she handled it so well and I was simply frozen. I wanted to tell her how proud I was of her - I wanted to hold her in my arms and cry with her. And the other thing that came from life's conditioning is pretending to be strong around the hospital staff and other families in the hospital. Not letting anyone see how devastated we were from his death. Even though he had a fatal diagnosis the grief and the shock is devastating!

Wrestling With Faith

It is normal for families to question God and faith during times of loss, tragedy, and grief. Some people may grow closer to God, while others may drift further away. Families need to know their feelings are valid and that every emotion is acceptable. It is okay to be angry with God, or to be confused about faith. He can handle it.

Susie -

After the devastation of the stillbirth last year, I found that I would pray probably 75 to 100 times each day for the twins, for over 5 months, waking in the night to pray as well. I don't understand why all the suffering, all the heartache, but I try to trust in the Lord and I try to be positive and think of when I will see them in heaven. It does not help much. I wanted to have them with their families here on earth. And then I feel guilty because God did not answer my prayers and I resent Him for that. And I dislike that a "friend" said to me, as the twins were fighting for life "the prayers of a righteous man availeth much." Bah, humbug, to that friend. That makes me either not righteous or not a man (and I don't think the Bible meant it that way, but more like "mankind").

When You Can't Pray
From The Sufficient Grace Blog (Kelly Gerken)

I am strong. I have to be strong. Women of faith don't fall apart. Because God is big. And, we must not have much faith, if we fall apart.

I remembered that lie, from years before I sat beside my mother's bed at the hospice center, whispered by the slithering one as I ran to the church restroom to hide the tears just weeks after I stood beside the tiny grave with the pink lined casket, the one holding my only daughters. Christians don't grieve without hope. My babies were in heaven. Didn't I believe enough? Why was this smothering grief knocking me over? **I am strong. I have to be strong. Women of faith don't fall apart.**

It was the same accusing lie when we heard the words incompatible with life in reference to our son, Thomas. Where is your God now? The voice questions, snarling. Stealing. Diminishing. Breaking. Twisting every truth, I clung to desperately.

Don't you have enough faith? What lesson didn't you learn the first time, that another child has to die? Why are you wrestling to find the answers... don't good Christians blindly trust and accept...don't those who are truly faithful never wrestle with doubt or fear? Don't they know all the answers?

I didn't even try to answer that time. I just wept over my bible.

The months I carried Thomas sucker punched my faith more, blow after blow. I just kept reading. And, I learned that being faithful doesn't mean not feeling doubt or fear. Faith is trusting God anyway... when you're most afraid and filled with doubt and questions. Believing when you don't see.

Those weeks in the hospice center, I sang to her. I read the Word to her. I prayed over her. I answered the questions of those around me. I was strong. Except for the day my baby brother had to carry me out, because I temporarily lost my mind to grief and exhaustion. Otherwise, I was strong. I had to be strong. That's what women of faith do, right?

I was a woman of faith. My God is big. Only, underneath, I was really more like the girl who had to be carried out by her baby brother as she fell to pieces in front of his eyes. After my mother died, when He finally took her home, I couldn't pray. For the first time in my life, I couldn't talk to the God who carried me.

I told my pastor, *"I can't pray right now. It's really bothering me. Every time I try to pray, I can't...all I can say is: 'I'm sorry God, I can't talk to you right now. It just hurts too much.'"*

My pastor said, ***"That's still prayer."***

I have thought of that truth often. And, many times, when grief is raw and you feel stripped naked, beaten to the core with the pain and disappointment of it all.... how. How could our God, our big loving Father God...let this happen? Why didn't He listen to our prayer? Was it because we aren't worthy... aren't enough... didn't pray right...didn't have enough faith? Why?

Grieving hearts ask those hard questions. I don't have all the answers; although, God has been patient to teach me many things in the surrendering and trusting, over the years. But, the longer I walk this journey, and the more brokenness I see along the way, I'm convinced that for some things, there are no answers this side of heaven. I can say all the words...and they're even true...those words...that God is good, that nothing separates us from His love, that He will never leave us nor forsake us...even in the darkest pits of despair. I can say them and I can promise that I've seen Him keep those promises in my own life. But, it won't take away the pain a heart feels when that which is most sacred has been ripped from her, and her heart lays in pieces at her feet.

Yes... it is a freeing, healing, soul-balming surrender to offer broken praise to heaven... and the sound is sweet to God's ears. He loves the broken praise. And, somehow showers healing back to us in the midst of the offering. But, if you can't muster it through the pain just yet.... if it hurts beyond words forming on lips. If you are just too hurt to talk to him right now, tell Him that much. Yell, scream, cry, sit there in silence.

That's still prayer.

He hears you, even when you can't utter the words. He hears the words of your broken heart, catches the falling tears in a bottle, and thinks of you more than the grains of sand on the longest beach. Even if you can't bear to talk to Him right now. Even if nothing He has allowed makes one ounce of human sense to your betrayed, broken heart. Even then, He holds you. He loves you. And, He fights for you.

And, that's still prayer.

The truth is, I am weak. My faith is small. But, my God, He is strong. And, my God is big. Big enough for my broken. And, big enough for your broken, too.

Understanding Perspective – Communication between Parents and Grandparents

Grandparents may grieve differently than parents. That can make it hard for them to understand the choices of their children (the parents of the baby). They may come from a generation or culture that does not believe you should see and hold your baby or get pictures. They may or may not understand the importance of creating those tangible memories. Grandparents often filter what they think is best through the lens of trying to protect their children, sometimes thinking that if they can just shield them from all of this, it won't hurt so badly. Parents spend their entire lives protecting their children. It makes sense that in the moment when their children experience the worst pain imaginable that they would want to find a way to protect them.

While most of what I share comes from the perspective of a grieving mother and one who provides support for family members grieving the loss of a baby or child, a recent experience has given me a greater level of compassion for grandparents. Two years ago, my youngest son, in his junior year of high school, lost one of his best friends in a tragic car accident. Xavier and his little brother Aidan were driving back to the high school after a routine dentist appointment when they went off the road and into a creek. The brothers, age 17 and 14 died in the accident. In an instant, their entire family and our close-knit community were changed forever.

Their parents lost both of their children. Their grandparents lost their grandsons, while agonizing over the unexplainable and irreparable pain of their own children. And, their classmates and teammates lost dear friends, promising students, all-American citizens, and all-star athletes. Everything stopped that day. The air was heavy with indescribable agony. Our community came together to walk with their family, and everyone in the region felt the weight of grief. Thousands traveled from miles around to pay their respects. Their parents found the strength to stand and greet everyone who came through the line as they stood beside the caskets of their beautiful sons.

When I received the call, I dropped the phone, sobbing painfully considering the pain of the boys' parents, our dear friends. My next thought was that I had to get to my son and his friends. In all my years of standing with people in grief, I have never witnessed such a massacre of emotional pain as walking through the halls of our beloved high school to find my son in the aftermath of a tragic accident that took the lives of two of "our" boys. Like every mother, I just needed to get to my kid. Everywhere, sobs and cries so filled with shock and utter despair. Sobs that matched my own when my husband said the words. Scanning the familiar tear-stained faces, searching for my own boy. Our community, rocked to its core.

When I found him, I did not want to let go.

In the initial days after the accident, I watched my son search for ways to honor the memory of the brothers. Their classmates planned a vigil, gathering our community in a moment when we all felt desperate and lost. My son led the vigil and hugged most of the attendees. His father and I stood in awe of the strength and grace God gave to our son and his friends in those days, so young to have lost the innocence and invincibility of youth. I held my breath, tears streaming down my face as I watched my son speak at the memorial service in our high school gymnasium, packed with thousands and over capacity. And, nothing could prepare us for the agony of watching our young teenage boys muster the strength to carry the caskets of their dearest friends.

While I would never attempt to compare the experience of watching my son feel such a depth of pain to a grandparent losing a grandchild, bearing witness to his grief and feeling helpless to ease it perhaps gave just the slightest window into a piece of the helplessness a grandparent feels while watching their own child grieve and not being able to ease the devastation. The days, weeks, and months after the accident left my son forever changed. Some days were filled with tears and songs played over and over as the hurt washed over his heart. Boys and men need to physically "do" in their grief. They need to do something tangible. Maybe build something, break something, paint a memorial, play a sport. They need to release the grief in various physical ways. Some days that looked like numbness, distance, anger, or frustration. He wanted to be around other people who understood exactly how he felt...and often, I was not included in that audience. The best I could do was to give him space when he needed it, and to be there whenever he did want me near to listen or to just sit with him in the brokenness.

Years ago, when I lost my twin daughters and later our newborn son, my own mother struggled in the weeks and months after our losses, wanting me to get better quickly. It was very hard for her not to be able to fix my pain. She worried that I was not being healthy when my grief took some time. She needed to understand that my pain was a healthy response to grief, and I needed her to be patient and present with me instead of trying to fix me. Communication on both ends and giving one another grace can help keep relationships intact.

Carla -
Yes. It (seemed to them) like this baby didn't exist. I want to remember her! I want to talk about how much I miss her. I want to talk about the fact that even though we did not hear her cry or get to look into her eyes, she was and is my granddaughter.

Cindi -
I refer to the babies by the names they were given even though we don't know their genders. I remember them each year on the day they were due. I want my daughter and son-in-law to know they will always be loved and never forgotten.

Anonymous -

My daughter-in-law pulled back from us. I know that this happened with her parents, too. She was so consumed by her grief. She and my son joined a bereaved parents' group and she saw a grief counselor. After about 9 months, she wrote me a letter that said that she had tried to pull away from everyone. She thought that would help her, but it didn't. She wanted us to know that she understood that she needed all of our support. I tried to find things to do to get her out of the house. We took a cake decorating class together. This was something I knew that she wanted to do. I drove 75 miles once a week to take the class with her. Let your children tell you what they need. Ask them. Give them space when they need it. Bring their favorite foods. Love them.

Lorrie -

During the first year or so after our granddaughter passed, it seemed that we couldn't do or say the right things, at the right times, to our grieving children, no matter how hard we tried. It seemed that we upset them often. We were frustrated and sad. They were angry and heartbroken. We finally understood and accepted that we were on a huge learning curve about grief, and that maybe we were the "safe place" for our children to express their anger at losing their sweet baby girl and having their world turned upside down. We let them know that we were sorry. We would try again and again to say and do the right things, and that we would always love them and always be there for them.

What Bereaved Parents Wish Grandparents Understood About Providing Support Through Grief

After reading some of the thoughts from the grandparents' perspective, we spoke with a few mothers about what they wished their parents knew about how to communicate with them after the loss of their baby. Many grandparents want to support their children as they walk through the pain of becoming a bereaved parent but may not know the best way to offer comfort. While some mothers shared the ways their parents comforted them in their grief, others struggled with the seeming lack of acknowledgement or connection from their parents. It was very important to most of the parents interviewed that the grandparents would remember their baby in future family rituals and celebrations.

Kara -

In the early days I didn't want to answer the phone or do any kind of talking. So my mom kept sending cards and kept it up for a long time. It was great because she found a way to share her love for me and my daughter, without me having to do anything. And then I kept them up until the next one would come to keep reading whenever I needed the pick me up.

She still does this for every birthday and angel birthday. The knowing someone else is remembering with me means the most.

Christina -

I wish my parents understood that it's not so easy to move on. That while most days we might seem okay, there a lot of moments where we hurt. The pain doesn't go away as easily as they think. While we know we have to move forward with our lives, I wish they understood it's not that easy. A lot of things trigger the pain.

Sara -

(I wish they would) acknowledge our babies in their count of grandchildren. My parents do. My in-laws will actually argue with us when we include Stephanie when asked how many children we have.

Cheryl -

My in-laws acknowledged her right after she was born, but most of the time now, they act like she didn't exist. They have also argued with me about how many kids we have. It hurts and is frustrating. I carried her, we love her, and we still miss her. I wish that they could understand that.

Erin -

My mother and my mother-in-law were amazing through the whole process! One of the things that stuck out to me the most with my mom, is the nurses took pictures of Rosalynn in the hospital. I was afraid to look at them for fear that she looked too "dead." My mom took the pictures and narrowed them down to the best. She helped take out the ones with amniotic fluid coming out of her nose and the unflattering ones.

We had had the baby shower a couple days before we lost Rosalynn. And because my husband is in the military, and was not home at the time, I laid everything out in the living room. When we went to the hospital because I had not felt her move, there was no way for me to know we weren't going to bring her home. My mom and mother-in-law and sister-in-law's went to my house cleared out the living room, the washer and dryer which had baby clothes in them, and put everything into the nursery and shut the door. Then they proceeded to clean my entire house.

The best thing though, is that even after almost 8 years, my mother still honors my daughter. She has a cherry blossom tree in her garden that blooms every year around the time that we lost her. She still openly talks about her and makes me feel comforted just hearing Rosalynn's name out of someone's mouth. She loves all of her grandchildren!

Being a mother now, to two beautiful girls here on Earth, I now know what my mother went through when I lost my daughter. You want to protect your children from every hurt and pain in the world. But that was one pain she could not protect me from! I cannot even imagine the pain that she went through knowing there was nothing she could do to help her daughter. That this was one pain she couldn't take away from me. People always say I'm so strong, and I'm one of the strongest people they know, but I give all of the credit for my strength and resilience to God and to my mother! I learned everything I am from her.

I shouldn't leave out my father!!! A man of very few words. Before we lost Rosalynn, we had a few things we wanted done around the house before she was born. For example, we wanted to build a mantel around our fireplace. Right after she passed, through the first month or two when I could barely get off the couch, *my dad would come over and tinker around the house. He built my fireplace mantel, that to this day I miss with all my heart because we had to leave it behind when we moved. Some of my best memories of that time are when I was sleeping on the couch, but I could feel dad's presence around the house. He would fix things and build things. I think it was his way of just being around me and making sure I was okay. He would let me cry, and just hold me, and never tried to say anything. He was just there! And now he is the most fantastic grandfather to all of his living grandchildren here on Earth!*

Mari -

So hard to put into words. My parents are amazing, have always been super supportive and overbearing at times... in a good way. They love hard and always go out of their way for my sister and me. Our daughter's stillbirth was extra hard because we are military and lived 14 hours from family and home. My mom was the first person I called as I was leaving the hospital with news our girl was no longer living and I'd have to be induced to deliver her. She immediately jumped into action and had my dad fly out to be with us and our living children (she was visiting my sister who is also married to a service member on the other side of the country). My parents helped handle all the funeral and burial arrangements since we were traveling to take our girl home to Texas.

Even though they didn't agree with how I reacted and handled a few things in my grief they have always been supportive and not pushy. They gave us space when needed and were there when needed. I will forever be grateful at how they have always included Ileana, they talk about and remember her like any of their living grandchildren and always include her. When people ask my mom about her grandbabies Ileana is always mentioned and remembered.

My in-laws were the complete opposite. When my husband called to tell them the news he was told "well, you can always try again", didn't come to funeral (live in different state), and never talk about her and change the subject when we bring her up. It almost feels as if they don't think of her as real because she never lived outside the womb. It's extremely hurtful and has put tension in that already strained relationship.

Paula -

I was too ill after our daughter's birth to plan the funeral. My parents took care of all the details for me and paid for it. The only thing me and my husband paid for was the headstone. To this day, I have no idea how much the funeral or plot cost (we only did a graveside funeral). I am eternally grateful for them taking care of the details that I was physically and mentally unable to do at the time.

My parents and in-laws do a very good job at remembering my kids as well, despite having several living grandchildren. I have always appreciated that. My mom gets me an owl and monkey ornament for the tree every year. And since I moved away, my mom also tends to the gravesite for me.

Amy -

My in-laws were supportive, but my parents weren't. My mom kept calling me and bugging me. She was very, very overbearing. Then they told me to put Benjamin's photos away when they came over to visit. His photos were only thing that help me through the grieving process. I love looking at his pictures. My parents never remember his birthday or ever mention his name for 5 years now. It is sad. I don't know if it is a cultural thing or not in their country. Also, my mom blamed me that it was my fault for losing him and that I didn't listen to her while pregnant. I know it isn't my fault.

My in-laws took care of the funeral and the gravesite. Benjamin was buried in the same plot on top of his great-grandfather. They often go to visit him when they can.

Sarah -

My parents returned stuff for me as well- baby gear, outfits, Christmas presents— it must have been so hard for them, but they didn't want me to have to do it.

Kirsten -

My parents were in from out of town when Philip was born. Because we were expecting him to come home within 1-2 weeks, everything in the house was ready- clothes washed, swing in living room, car seat ready to go, etc. When we lost him, they stayed at my house and when I walked in the door everything was moved- it looked as if we had never been expecting a Baby. They had put everything in storage, in a closet, or in our basement. It really upset me, but I didn't know how to tell them that- "I already didn't have my son to bring home and now everyone had shoved him away in a closet as if he never existed". Some people might like this, but I wish they would have at least asked.

They moved forward a lot faster than I did and stopped counting my son as a grandchild within months. This still hurts to this day. It might be reality but it's hard to try to "force" people to remember that there should be one more. It is always special when they do remember to count him in "8 grandchildren and one in heaven" but not as often as I'd like.

Last thing I can think of is they pushed really hard for me to be on antidepressants about 6 weeks after losing him. I had enough to process without people pushing me- part of my own healing was being able to feel the deep sadness of losing my son. I needed their support not their opinions. I don't mean to sound rude, but it just felt like they wanted me to be "better" as if this had never happened. They couldn't understand.

Charmel -

My daughter, Emilia, was born asleep on March 15, 2017 at 33 weeks gestation. What did my parents/in-laws do that was supportive during and after the loss of Emilia? My biggest fear is that Emilia will be forgotten, but I have learned that will never happen. My parents have helped us to keep Emilia's memory alive in several different ways. They regularly mention her name and include her in the family just as they honor each of their living grandchildren. One of the frustrations of being a bereaved parent is the non-acknowledgement we often receive during the death of our child. Remembering special dates and mentioning our child's name is the greatest gift anyone can give. One way my parents went over and beyond was by creating a scholarship in memory of our daughter, The Emilia Madeleine Rose Clough Scholarship. Each year this scholarship is funded and awarded by my parents in memory of Emilia. They have been supportive of my husband and I in every step we take to honor our child. They have become active within their own communities to advocate for pregnancy and infant loss.

What did my parents/in-laws do or not do that was not helpful during the loss of Emilia? As a parent myself, I know how hard it is to watch your child struggle. To see them going through something difficult and wanting so badly to "fix" things for them. When we loss Emilia, I felt like our parents were trying to "fix us." Our parents tried to provide the perfect words that could instantly make us feel better to remove our grief. My in-laws would try to give explanations to justify why Emilia died which often hurt us more than anything. After Emilia died, my parents and mother-in-law (who live out of state) visited us in the hospital every day and helped us celebrate Emilia's life at her visitation. My father-in-law, however, was absent. He never met Emilia and the lack of interest in wanting to be present for his child and grandchild pained us. As a child, I know our parents want to be here for us. We know they don't intentionally do or say things to hurt us. We also know that they would go to the ends of the world to take our grief away.

As a bereaved parent, I don't expect anyone to try to take my grief away. Just acknowledge my grief, my child, and the love that I will always have for her. There are no words that will ever be shared that can begin to take away the pain of living life without Emilia. Instead of offering advice, explanations, and justifications for why she died; just sit with me, hold me, cry with me, and remember with me the life of my daughter that I will forever love.

Miracle -

My parents accompanied us to every single trip to the funeral home so we wouldn't have to go alone, except for when we picked up our baby's ashes because we needed to do that alone. They also had us stay at their house the night he passed away so we wouldn't have to go home to an empty house. They have paid for funeral costs and food and helped us with getting back on our feet while mourning and let us decide the best way to handle things and never pushed us to do things we weren't ready for or didn't want to do. They were 100% behind us and still are.

They also handled all the stuff for letting people know about the funeral and memorial service and sent out all the thank you notes for all the gifts and help we received so we wouldn't have to.

Kristy -

My parents were there at the hospital with me the entire day I was being induced and came back the next morning with our pastor to pray over our son and as we said goodbye to leave the hospital. Having them there was incredible. Most of my side of the family came, all of my siblings & their spouses. Being surrounded by them to talk, pray, cry, and prepare our hearts to deliver our son was so precious to us. After he was delivered, everyone was able to hold him. Unfortunately, it was a bit of deja vu as we had done the same for my younger sister when one of her twin boys was not expected to live more than a few minutes after birth. My family is not afraid to say my son's name or my nephew's. My husband's family doesn't talk about it at all.

My parents bought us a wind chime with a bible verse on it to hang outside in honor of our son & my mom still checks on me frequently. ♥

Instead of offering advice, explanations,
and justifications for why she died,
just sit with me, hold me, cry with me,
and remember with me the life of my child,
whom I will forever love.

Charmel – Emilia's Mother

Bethany -

Wanted to give you feedback about what my parents did that was so healing for us. I know each child is different, but I truly felt like I didn't get to celebrate Lillian as I should have been able to.

My mom either just listened to the Lord or her instincts. She bought me a balloon and flowers and a card for a baby girl. I wanted and needed that.

She was very sensitive to say her name and each week- and still. To this day she does this. 4 years later!!! She celebrates Lillian's birthday day each month and remembers how many months she would be. It still truly blesses me.

My father made a necklace for Lillian that we got to embrace and cry together with and over and honor her. I even got a picture of it on her hand to give him that following Father's Day.

They were just very supportive. And cooked meals and just let us lead the way in grieving. They honor her and celebrate her which is what I needed them to do. And it was rare probably, but knowing your own child is knowing how to help grieve alongside them I feel.

Now my in-laws. They hurt me. They never said anything and even acted like she was never born. I know they didn't know but I even emailed them to give them permission to celebrate her. Talk about her etc.

I don't know what else to do, but I couldn't stand to be around them due to this. But then my mother in love lost her husband that following year. And she then began celebrating her and including her and talking more. That has been such a sweet gift I cherish very much.

Talking. Honoring. Including. Crying with. Celebrating with. Looking at pictures etc. those are all what we want from our parents. Support and remembering those are healing.

Amie -

Even though we knew our daughter would not survive, my parents sent us roses to congratulate her birth. And every year since, they've sent us the same bouquet on her birthday. It's really touching and is something I look forward to every year.

Lauren -

My parents came and stayed with us for a week. I felt like it was too long and added stress because I felt the need to entertain and had a delay in the time to grieve in my own way. There were a few times I specifically requested to be left alone and my mom would not leave me alone. I know she was trying to help, but I really just needed some time to myself. I guess my advice would be that if your child is able to voice what they want/need, respect what they are asking for.

Sarah -

My parents were wonderful and supportive and still are. We don't speak to my in-laws so not sure if they even care.

My mom and dad have said it is so difficult to see us hurting, especially seeing me hurting and not being able to do anything for us. They talk about Ella every day and have her picture up at their house. They count her as one of their grandchildren as we do when we talk about our children.

The only thing that was hard is in the beginning when my mom kept talking about the what if's. I had to tell her she couldn't do that if she wanted me to heal.

Also, another thing that is hard is when I say how sad I am, and she says we all are- which is true, but I sometimes feel like it takes away from the pain I am feeling.

44

Heather -

My mom and I lived 7 hours apart in two different states. She dropped everything and drove halfway across the state when I told her I was pretty sure I was in labor. When contractions slowed down, instead of driving home, she got a hotel room where she was, and 7 hours later when we went to the hospital, she finished the drive to be there when my son was born.

My in-laws kept our oldest son most of the night after school (full-day preschool) until his dad got off work. I was neither physically nor emotionally able to keep up with him, especially on dad's late night. So, their support meant we were able to get through it with our son.

My mother-in-law helped me prepare the most beautiful reception after the funeral. I was sad that I wasn't going to be able to make him a birthday cake like I had done every year for my older son, and told her that I wanted to celebrate his life, make him a birthday cake and cupcakes and cookies... all frog themed since that was the animal we picked out. Her momma had been a cake decorator and everything my MIL knew about cake decorating she learned from her mom and had been teaching me. To help pass the time after he was born, we baked and decorated over 100 cookies and cupcakes with frogs and made a giant frog cake. She set up the dessert table at the church, so everything was absolutely beautiful and perfect for celebrating him.

Putting away Christmas stuff today and I was reminded of how much a part of our family Riley is. On our first Christmas without him, my MIL saw an ornament with his name in it. She bought it and gifted it to me to hang on the tree every year. My in-laws are making a memorial garden on the family farm for him, and he is never far from hearts and minds when we are together. They feel the hole that losing a grandchild has left and they have done so much to help us find ways to create memories where the hole doesn't feel quite so big and he feels included.

Amber -

In response to your question regarding what you wish your parents did/didn't do: I was blessed to have support from both sets of parents in that they both offered tremendous support. One of the biggest things is that they remembered my babies; they used their names. They never pretended like it didn't happen. It is a part of my story, so it became a part of their story. They listened... when I needed to vent about ANOTHER pregnancy announcement or when it was trigger dates or whatever. Some tangible/specific things my baby's grandparents did: gave us money for dinner in the early days of our grief; gave us an Etsy gift card to buy something to remember our babies; gave us remembrance ornaments; went to support groups with me or encouraged me to go; gave my living daughter books for siblings of pregnancy loss; bought rocks for our local remembrance garden. The main thing though that has meant the most is just being there and giving us time... not trying to minimize our grief and not trying to rush us or push us to get pregnant again.

Supporting Parents as They Grieve

- Offer to help cover the cost of memorial services if you're able.

- Give parents opportunities to connect by offering to watch other children or helping to pay for the cost of a night out or a weekend getaway.

- Make or order a tangible comfort item, such as a prayer blanket or shawl.

- Resist the urge to rush your son or daughter through their grief and healing. Be patient with them and allow them the time they need to walk through grief.

- As you find ways to process your emotions and heal through your own grief, find your own separate support person to talk to. While it is okay to feel and cry with your son or daughter, avoid putting the weight of your own grief on their already sagging shoulders.

Remembering & Including Your Grandchild in Family Traditions

As time goes by, know that it will mean so much to the child's parents if you continue to find ways to honor and include the memory of your grandchild in family celebrations and when you are doing things for your living grandchildren. It is typically a comfort if you remember with them.

- Don't be afraid to speak their names. Parents want to know that you remember the baby with them. One of the biggest fears mothers especially share is that their baby will be forgotten. It will be a comfort to your son or daughter that you will include their baby and remember their baby with them.

- Include baby in holiday celebrations. An ornament for the tree in memory of their baby, a keepsake at Easter, acknowledgment on Mother's Day and Father's Day, a Valentine for their heavenly baby.

- Display something that represents their baby along with pictures of your living grandchildren. Even if you are not comfortable displaying a picture, something that represents their baby will still be a comfort.

- Buy a piece of memorial jewelry or a gift card for parents to purchase something to remember their little one.

Helpful Ways to Offer Comfort and Support to Grieving Grandparents

Be Sensitive to a Grandparent's Compounded Grief Story

The experience of watching their child give birth to a baby with a brief life or one who is born still may trigger memories of their own loss and missed opportunities. If you are present with a grieving grandparent, please be sensitive to their own stories. They may be processing grief that's been repressed for years as they hold their grandbaby. Allow them an opportunity to process their grief for the child they lost as well as the grief they're feeling for the loss of their grandchild and the pain their child is feeling.

Dawn -

We were supported by family and friends and our church family. At that point nothing was a comfort to me. I honestly don't know what I would've found helpful. After several months under psychiatric care I found SGM (Sufficient Grace Ministries), and they welcomed me and gave me a place to share what I was feeling with others who get it! Because we all know if you haven't been there you DON'T get it. Even though I didn't really fit with this group of younger mommas who had lost their babies during pregnancy or shortly after, and I being a grandma who lost a 2 year old, they welcomed me anyway and I believe it may have saved me. I started to feel a bit of hope again.

Anita -
My co-workers just appeared, one by one. My husband and brother had to drive from 2 hours away. Firefighters went to find him on the road and pick him up. Support from the hospital staff was very lacking.

Sarah -
Yes, Sufficient Grace Ministries was there and took great pictures and gave Kristy many keepsakes. Seeing our daughter comforted by this brought comfort to us. Yes, the ladies from SGM included our entire family and there were a lot of us there. They were so helpful with advice and encouragement.

Vicki -
What would help people in my situation would be open, honest discussions regarding pregnancy, infant, child loss. To remove the stigma and understand that it's not only the parents who are lost! Grandparents require support as well because most of us are over the moon to learn we'll become grandparents and to then lose that dream in the physical sense is devastating; add that to watching your child go through unfathomable pain that cannot be assuaged. It is painful, overwhelming, and nearly impossible to survive intact.

Cathy -
I took pictures of our sweet babies that I will always treasure.

Joi -
I think my situation was unique because my daughter and her family live 8,000 miles away. So, when I returned to the states after Ezekiel's two short weeks of life, it felt like I was alone in my grief and it seemed that no one knew the great loss I had experienced. There was no memorial service to attend here with my family or church friends, no grave site to visit as a place to go to

grieve and barely any acknowledgement by my workplace. I searched Facebook and other social media looking for support for grieving grandparents. Our church is very small, so I was hoping to find a group to join to be able to talk about Ezekiel and my grief --- grief over his loss and grief for the unbearable pain my daughter was going through. I joined a few FB groups and shared a little about my grief, but my heart could not stand reading about the hurt of the other grieving mothers, imagining that was how my daughter was hurting or they did not share the Christian perspective on death that I cling to and therefore offered me no comfort. My husband, Ezekiel's grandfather, had only "met" Ezekiel one time through a brief video chat during one of my short visits to the PICU. While he was supportive of me and a good listener, he didn't share the intensity of grief that I felt -- was that because he is a male or because he didn't experience what I did?? --- I don't know. I wish I could have talked to other grieving grandmothers to see what they experienced. My greatest comfort came from Scripture, listening to music that was theologically sound which spoke His comfort to my heart (Sovereign Grace music), and talking/texting with a very close friend who loved me through all my emotions of grief without judgment. My husband and I also had a large stone made as a remembrance stone with Ezekiel's name, birth date and going Home date on it. We placed that large stone by a large oak tree in our front yard and I gaze at it whenever I come and go to our home. It is a special place for me to go to remember Ezekiel and marvel at his precious life and wonder what he is experiencing in heaven.

Anonymous -

We were present when our granddaughter was born an angel. Our minister drove 75 miles in a rainstorm to baptize her. The ceremony was very touching and everyone including the minister cried for all that we had lost. We know that our granddaughter is truly an angel and that we will see her one day. My daughter-in-law saved some of the holy water. She was given a certificate of baptism and a cross. Such precious mementos of this sweet little girl.

Both the chaplain and the nurses were so supportive. The nurses were wonderful and clipped some of the baby's hair and did plaster hand and footprints. They also did inked foot and handprints. There is one plaster thumb print with my son and daughter-in-law's thumbs in the shape of a heart with my granddaughter's handprint above it. My daughter-in-law has a memento box for her first daughter. She also ordered a bereavement bear that is the same weight as my granddaughter when she was born. I finished the afghan and gave it to my son and daughter-in-law. I know that my daughter-in-law hugged that afghan for comfort. I contacted an organization called "Minutes of Gold". There wasn't anything other than the usual receiving blankets to wrap my granddaughter in. We made do, but I found that "Minutes of Gold" donates outfits and afghans for stillborn babies. That would have been such a comfort. Since I contacted them, they donated 18 sets of outfits and afghans in our granddaughter's memory to the hospital where she was born an angel.

Karen -
    When we were with our son and daughter-in-law at the funeral home helping to plan the service, the director brought in the information about Sufficient Grace Ministries. The tiny blue burial gown was so beautiful. The Comfort Bear was so soft and precious. Immediately we all felt comforted, knowing that there was an organization that was very close to our location that was willing to help our family. SGM has become a very important part of our family.

Cindi -
    I felt well supported by a good friend of mine who had lost her teenage son 20+ years before I met her. When I got the news Bentley had no heartbeat I was an emotional wreck. She came to my house, brought me a plant, prayed and cried with me. I also got sympathy cards from some people which meant a lot because it validated the fact that this was a loss of a baby not just a medical issue. I wish I could have found a support group for grieving grandparents. I searched everywhere on the internet and found nothing dealing with the loss of grandchildren through miscarriage. 5wk, 11 wk

51

Vickie O. -

We were very fortunate to have a friend of a friend come to help. She had experienced a stillbirth herself 5 months earlier. She was a nursing student. Her baby had been born in the same hospital room and my grandson was using the Cuddle Cot that she and her husband had donated. She was an absolute angel and not only shared her experience but gave us suggestions of things to do to create memories. My son made a cast of him holding his son's hand. They dressed him. Kept him in their room for 3 days. Her message was to make the time you have count. Make memories. This new friend and her advice made all the difference. We were lost. She showed up, shared our grief, then gave us direction. Make memories. Take pictures. Dress your baby. Clean your baby. Take casts that will be lifelong physical proof that your child was here.

Susie -

No, I never felt well-supported. Only a couple of close friends seemed to try to understand at all, and that took awhile. People say terrible things because they don't know what to say, they have misconceptions, and they think they know all about it when they don't. The worst ones are from friends and acquaintances who say things such as "God knows best", "God needed another angel." Or sometimes people say "there must have been a reason," "well, at least they have two children" (one of the daughters) or "they can try again" (the childless couple - although they are not really childless; their twins are not with them but in heaven). When the stillborn baby was born, we received many cards. Not nearly as many with the twins. Sometimes I feel like a pariah - with many people staying clear of me. Also, I feel many people think that since the other four were so little somehow they did not count. Each baby was so longed for, each loss was heartbreaking and crushing, and each and every baby is unique. We live in a fallen world where bad things happen to good people, but it seems like we have had way too many heartbreaking baby losses in our family.

Tracy -

I did have comfort from friends and family. I also took comfort in my church. I cried all the way from Newark to Seattle and I prayed it was wrong and Mya would be delivered alive. I was angry at God, but I kept praying. Right after I called a friend of mine, Father Vincent, and told him how angry I was at God and he said I had every right to be. He really helped me with my grief at that time. The biggest comfort was just saying her name to people, I don't know why but it did.

Grandpa -

Yes, that time was very meaningful. There was a Now I Lay Me Down to Sleep photographer at each hospital. They were wonderful. The second hospital helped with hand molds and foot/hand molds. We treasure these things as a family. These things were very helpful.

It was helpful but I wouldn't say well-supported. It was a comfort to just spend time with Samuel. We tried with all our power to get to bring Samuel's body back to the hospital that our daughter was at because she had not had a chance to hold him. They would not let us. We found out later that it would have happened if we talked to the right people. Our daughter was heartbroken.

Sharla -

I didn't feel supported at all. I felt utterly alone and lost, questioning God... why? My faith had been shattered yet my faith ended up being my comfort. Without God I would have never made it. Having my daughter and son-in-law move in with us after she was released from the hospital brought me comfort... to be able to care for my daughter as I did when she was a little girl. I believe the nurses at the hospital where my daughter gave birth to Lily needed more training concerning stillbirths and grief. They did what they could and knew I guess but still were lacking.

What Grieving Grandparents Wish Friends, Family, and Caregivers Understood

Losing a child or grandchild changes a person, and along with that comes changes in our relationships with friends and relatives. Every grieving parent or family member I have met has been hurt by the words of someone else. Sometimes those words were well-intentioned from someone who was supposed to love the broken-hearted griever. Some words don't seem to have been thought out at all or may come from the heart of one who is bitter and hurting. I think that most people do not intend to bring harm with their words. It is just difficult to know how to comfort someone who is walking through intense grief, especially if you have not experienced great loss in your own life.

I have been a grieving mother...a mother who has walked this path. A mother who has heard the hurtful words. A mother who had some friends who just couldn't be around me. Friends who didn't want to hear about my babies. Friends who didn't understand my loss. (I also have wonderful friends who did love me, pray for me, cry with me and come alongside me. They were few in number, but they exist. We have many friends who support our efforts to reach out to others, now. But the early days were lonely.) And yet, I have also inadvertently said insensitive things to a mother who had several losses. Not knowing of her struggle to have children, and the heart ache of the losses she had endured, I said something about what a great dad her husband would be. She looked at me as if I had stabbed her in the heart. And, in fact...my words had done just that. Did I intend to harm her? No, absolutely not. But, I did, unknowingly. And, I of all people should know that we never know where someone has walked. We never know what they have endured...what they may be suffering. We should be careful with our words.

While talking with another mom who has lost a child, she asked me what she should say to a mom who had just lost her young baby. She was delivering a Dreams of You Basket to her. She and I both knew the answer at the same time....

There are no words. Just hug her. Maybe say you are sorry. Offer her your love and prayers. The reason it is so hard to say the right thing...the reason so many people say the wrong thing...is because in reality, there are no words. There are no words that can comfort the ache - the canyon of sorrow. None.

My lovely friend Dawn, from Marshall Photography made a great point regarding the way friends can offer support to someone who is grieving.

Dawn wrote:

"And when they raised their eyes from afar, and did not recognize him, they lifted their voices and wept, and each one tore his robe and sprinkled dust on his head toward heaven. So they sat down with him on the ground seven days and seven nights, and no one spoke a word to him, for they saw that his grief was very great." Job 2:12-13

If only his comforters had continued what they started and simply stayed by Job's side, instead of trying to explain or give counsel. How many times we try to do things in love…and in the end, we screw it up.

She and I shared a conversation about her comment. She talked about Job's friends…and the fact that they just sat with Job in his grief for seven days. They wept with him. They just stayed beside him. They were willing to walk with him…but they said nothing. They were so supportive during that time. Now, we all know that Job's friends fell short after that. But when did they get into trouble? When did they cease to be a comfort to Job? When they opened their mouths to speak in judgment of Job. What a powerful example to us as we consider how to support someone who is in raw grief.

Sometimes, well-meaning friends want to rush a grieving heart toward quick healing. They just want us to be better or to return to the person we used to be before the loss. Sometimes in their efforts to find something helpful or hopeful to say, they may inadvertently say something insensitive that diminishes our pain. Any phrase that beings with "at least" or that tries to refocus us from our pain to the silver lining, is not helpful in raw grief. In those moments of early grief, I just needed someone to weep with me, pray for me, and walk with me. Someone to get it. Someone who wasn't afraid to sit with me awhile in the pain.

As we emerge as that new person, we are different in many ways. Perspective changes. What once seemed so important no longer matters. It is replaced with things you never thought much about before, but now realize matter a great deal. While we will heal and joy will be restored in our lives, we are forever changed. Our very personality may even change. And, we will never get over losing our children or grandchildren. Not that we wallow in grief forever. Not that we will not be fully healed and complete. We will, but we will have a missing place in our hearts until we reach heaven's welcoming gates. A place where a much loved, dearly cherished, longed for and dreamed about life once lived. Now that life lives on in heaven…the place that we are homesick for, at times. Our children and grandchildren will forever be part of the tapestry of our lives…they are part of who we are. We can no more deny them, than we could our children who walk this earth with us.

Lynnette Kraft writes:

Right after Anna died I desperately needed somebody who had lost a child to tell me I'd be okay. I was so sick with grief that I didn't feel I'd ever recover. I couldn't imagine ever being truly happy again without Anna…it just didn't seem possible. That somebody never came. I did recover though. God was all I really needed. My joy did return. God did turn my mourning into dancing.

How we long for someone to understand how we feel when we are trying to navigate through the thick fog of early grief. We asked the grandparents to share what they wished others understood about what it is like to be a grieving grandparent.

Vicki -

They are REAL babies! Knowing you can get pregnant but don't get to have a living baby is no consolation. And saying it to me because they are my grandchildren instead of my children is unacceptable. Do not shy away from me because of this; meet me where I am and offer me comfort even if it is silent company that allows me to cry openly. Understand that I need to grieve my grandsons as much as I needed to grieve my mother when she passed. Maybe even more so because I had 48 wonderful years with her to look back on, but I have no memories made with them to comfort me now.

Patty -

It leaves a hole in your heart so deep and understand we count our grandchild that have passed in our total amount of grandchildren we have.

Sarah -

Don't be afraid to speak their name, don't be afraid to smile or laugh from their memories, don't be afraid to go on. "Never say goodbye because goodbye means going away and going away means forgetting."- Peter Pan

Our pain is doubled. Our baby has lost their baby. The pain is indescribable, your baby looks to you for comfort and you have no idea how to fix it.

Jo -

I don't think you can understand it unless you've walked it, so I hope they never understand it. Being there means more than I think anyone understands. Those friends of mine who came to Areille's funeral were like a balm to my soul. I know it was hard for them, I didn't ask them, I was so wrapped up in my son and daughter-in-law and so worried about them. I had no idea or energy to reach out, but my friends reached out to me and I have never been happier to see their faces!

Anita -

Time does dull the pain. I had to take photos down early on because I just couldn't take it. The pictures in my head and in my heart were all I could deal with. I still can't watch videos or hear his voice, but that will come, I imagine. It has just been over a year so seeing little ones at the store, or in restaurants is still painful at times but I know our baby is in the arms of God and I will see him again!

It is no less painful because we are the grandparents. We grieve for our child and try to help them survive the loss, and we grieve our own loss of our grandchild. It's a double whammy.

Cathy -
As above, these babies were our grandchildren as much as any living grandchildren. It is okay for others to talk about their pending grandchildren because all babies are precious. Acknowledge the short life and lost potential of our babies. Don't ignore their memory.

Sarah -
It hurts a lot, we lost 2 grandchildren, Ryan at birth and Vance at 20 weeks. Your heart hurts twice as much because you see your child hurting over the loss of their child and your heart breaks because your grandchild has passed on. Only another grandparent can understand the depth of your grief, it's so real and painful. Even as I type this the tears are running down my face.

Joi -
I just wish people would not forget so quickly. It has been a little over a year since my grandson died and 1-2 friends still ask me how I'm doing or ask how my daughter is doing or say something about Ezekiel and show that they have not forgotten him or my loss. It doesn't have to be anything earth shattering, just ignore any feelings of awkwardness you may have and let a grieving grandparent know they are still on your heart. A grieving grandparent would definitely prefer those feelings of awkwardness over feelings that their great loss has been forgotten!

Debbie -
I wish people understood that we are grieving as well, we suffered a loss, we are feeling lost, alone and empty.

Karen -
When people ask me how many grandchild we have, I always tell them that we have 5 living and one in Heaven. It's important for people to know that we always include him as part of our family. I'm looking forward to being Grandma to him when I get "home" to Heaven someday.

Lisa -

You don't get over it. You aren't doing better with time. We need to talk about our loss and our grandchild, no matter how long they were with us. They are still a part of our lives.

Cindi -

That this is the loss of a grandchild that I loved. Asking if my daughter has other children does not make this child less valuable.

Carole -

I wish they understood how deep and all-consuming the pain is, double dose in a way. Be patient and kind, and understand that the loss of a child no matter their age or time on earth is the most heartbreaking thing that anyone can go through, and that pain continues with all the first milestones that you never get to share, first birthday, first smile etc etc. Talk with the grieving grandparent about the child, and don't look shocked and walk away when they need to include their grandchild in the conversation.

Rick -

Be fully present. Don't try to answer the unanswerable. Don't try to fix anybody - you can't. Keep taking care of yourself so that you can remain fully present with and for your kids. Ask two questions. 1) How are you doing? 2) How can I help?

Words are overrated and tend to hurt more than help. Love is in the small actions and in faithfulness.

Vickie O. -

Be very aware of what you say. If you've heard it said a hundred times before, best not say it. "Everything happens for a reason". That kind of crap is not good. Just be there. Let them know you love them. Grieve with them. Read. There are lots of good writings. And just know that this is one of the hardest experiences you will ever endure. You will have to be strong for your child and do what they cannot do for themselves. I took over planning the memorial service when my son and his partner couldn't think straight. We made it happen and it was beautiful. After it was over my son thanked me for making it happen. The truth was, I never wanted to plan a memorial service for my grandson. No one does. But I knew it had to happen. They have so many friends that wanted to honor their child and share their grief. The memorial gave us a time to share and honor their child.

Susie -

Losing a baby grandchild is not like losing a loved one with whom you have had a relationship. With the death of a baby you lose "what might have been." The much anticipated child is wrenched away by death, and you have no memories to fall back on like you do with an older person. You have lost a great part of your life. You have lost all the "this little piggies" and lullabies that choke in your throat even thinking of them.

You have also lost your daughters, who will never recover. And your sons-in-law. And your other grandchildren who are so affected. The ripple effect is immense and overwhelming. And people may ask the baby's mother how she is doing, treat her with concern, help in other ways -- but everyone else is pretty much ignored as not being a part of the loss. The daddies, the grandmas and grandpas, the aunts and uncle, the other children - siblings and cousins - all grieve too. Yes, the mother was the one holding that baby in her body, giving birth, preparing to nurse. But the daddy was excited, and helped create that baby and helped the mother during her pregnancy. Helped share the dreams of what was to be. And the siblings would feel the baby move, kiss that baby through mommy's tummy, and whisper their love and desire for when "baby" would be with them. Please understand that grief extends to ALL the family. And please acknowledge that the loss of that baby has changed everyone.

As the grandma of 7 babies now in heaven, I still weep every day and every night for them - and for my family. I ask the Lord to let them know how much they are loved and missed by their families, and by me. They are never out of my mind. I talk to them as I go to bed, I sing lullabies, and when I visit a grave by myself,

I sometimes read a book and sing if I can, or think it in my head if I can't. I love my grandchildren - all 10 of them. Please also understand that I have something similar to panic attacks when I see babies, even when I walk past the diaper aisle in a store, and that I simply cannot go to baby showers yet - and maybe never. Please understand that I am happy when your children have babies, but looking at pictures is like stabbing a knife and twisting it in my heart. And I don't know how to answer when you say, "we are up to 10 grandkids now, how about you guys?" I am up to 10 now too, but only 3 to play with, to visit, to buy Christmas and birthday gifts for. "All the babies die" - yes, I am blessed to have 3 living grandchildren. They are wonderful. But oh, I wonder what their lives would be like if their "babies" had lived. One little boy would not be an only child wishing there was someone to play with. And they all would have new baby twin cousins. But it did not happen. And I wonder if life will ever be happy again. I long for those days before all these deaths. I want to rewind life. I want to return to when life was happy. But that isn't how it works.

Just be patient with me. I am hurting. And the hurt festers. And no, I will never be who I used to be. Quit telling me that the Lord knows best. Quit telling me about when you lost your baby but that it will all be fine soon. I have lost more than my baby. I have lost my family because we are all changed. We love each other, but we are different. We still can have good times, but every family picture has seven children missing. There are big holes in our family. And good times together don't fill in those holes; there is always the elephant in the room, always the knowledge that we are missing out, always thoughts of the ones in heaven. Those holes will always remain.

Karen -

Any grief is difficult for people to understand unless they have experienced it themselves. Others should not judge or put expectations on those that grieve. Walk alongside the grieving person, hold their hand and their heart. Grief as a grandparent is heartbreaking as your child is suffering and there is nothing, absolutely nothing, that you can do to make that suffering go away. Along with those emotions and feelings, you are grieving the loss of your grandchild, your baby's baby. Such a difficult time, so many emotions.

Rita -
    This was Hayley's baby and in our hearts he was our baby, too. Xander came into this world and he left quickly. He was here. Please don't compare your experiences with this one. What matters at this moment is our loss, not yours. At least not at this time. Grief can be very painful so less words are more words. Give all of us your prayers, love and hugs.

Kathy T. -
    Although our grandchild never grew his/her first tooth or took his/her first step... doesn't make us less of a grandparent. ♥

Dave and Mary Jo -
    How absolutely debilitating it is for a very, very long time. Your world loses its color and joy. You live in this gray space, separated from real life as if in another time and space for a long time. You think you should be able to get over it but you don't for a long, long time. Think in years, not weeks or months. You slowly begin to carry the grief with you tucked deep inside your heart. It will pop up from time to time and you have to stop and let it come but then you tuck it back in and carry it some more. We are quite certain for the rest of our life. We miss what should have been so much. There is always a little boy that is missing from our day in and day out life here on earth. We long for heaven and the forever that we will have with him someday.

Maria -
    Speaking as a bereaved grandparent and as a widow, don't be afraid of a grieving person's tears. Don't be afraid to mention their loved one's name. In almost every case, they would rather cry when you talk about their loved one, instead of crying because no one remembers. Either way they will cry, but it helps to know that people remember him or her. I read this quote recently: "If you know someone who has lost a very important person in their life,

and you're afraid to mention it because you think you may make the person sad by reminding them of someone who died—you're not reminding them; they didn't forget. What you're reminding them of is that you remembered that the person lived. And that is a great, great gift." (Lost & Found Grief Center)

Janella -

Don't be afraid you'll only cry when you meet your grandchild. Though saying goodbye is painful, saying hello is the most precious gift you will receive. Enjoy the hello! Hello is beautiful! There is love and joy along the journey. Celebrate that!

Facing grief is always a challenge. Facing grief as a grandparent is, well, I'm not sure how to say it. You always want to protect your children. This time, you cannot just make it all better. Watching your daughter bury her child will break you on many levels. As a grandparent, you just want to fall apart, but can't. You are needed by so many people on so many levels. We have eight kids. They all needed me. Our oldest granddaughter needed us too. And I simply felt like I wasn't enough for everyone. Just take the time to ask them to tell you about the grandchild they will have to say goodbye to too soon. If they are like me, they will want to share everything they can about the grandchild they won't be able to watch grow.

Pat -

Honor your grandchild. Celebrate their angelversary by visiting their grave, send up balloons, talk about them. Rosalyn was part of our lives for 37 weeks. We were overjoyed, excited, loved her and couldn't wait for her... she was a big part of our lives and always will be. We have all learned from her and she continues to teach us 7 years later. She is our little angel.

This lasts a lifetime... it gets easier, but I can never forget her pretty little face, her little fingers, her hair... and when I held her, she was limp. Those memories never go away.

From One Grandparent's
Heart to Another

We asked grandparents what they would say to another grandparent walking through the loss of their grandchild. No one can understand what you are experiencing better than someone who has walked this path. Many grandparents carry the weight of their own grief in silence, as they are more focused on easing their child's suffering. Your grief is valid, and you have a right to process and feel your pain as well. Below are responses from the hearts of other grieving grandparents. Grab a cup of coffee or tea and sit with them a minute. It is my prayer that their words will help you feel a little less alone and unseen on this journey.

Kristi -
That it's not only a loss for your children... but a loss for you too. That it's okay to talk about it. It's okay to mourn and it's okay to laugh.

Sarah -
Mourn with your child, don't pretend all is well. Help out however you can and spend time with God.

Joi –
To other bereaved grandparents -- I really don't know what to say!... except cling to Christ! You will desire to do the comforting

and to take away the pain of your child as they walk through their grief, but that's not your job.... that is the job of the Holy Spirit, our Comforter. Your job is to support your child in their journey through all the emotional turmoil of grief, without judgment, to listen with patience and understanding, to lift them often in prayer, to love unconditionally, to help them meet their physical needs (food, childcare, rest) as much as possible and to hopefully help them carry their tremendous burden of grief.

Debbie -
There will always be an empty space that nothing and no one can fill. We were blessed last month when my son and daughter-in-law gave birth to a healthy beautiful baby girl but the void of Francis is still there. Hold the memory of your grandbaby in your heart. Talk about the baby often, if not with the child's parents, find a friend, a pastor, or a support group.

You, as a grandparent, lost a child as well. The pain and grief is real whether the child was able to take a breath or not, it is still your grandbaby. Find a way to honor the memory. For me it was a tattoo, for some it may be to plant a tree or a garden. Don't be afraid to cry and share your pain, especially with your child. Let your child know that you are there for them and you are grieving with them. Keeping silent may make them feel that you aren't grieving. Hold that baby in your heart till the day you can hold them in your arms.

Karen -
Grieving over the loss of a grandchild was one of the hardest times I've had to experience in my life. A strong family support system and the belief that God was with us, even during this nightmare, helped greatly. We have our faith in God, and we know that we will all see Him in Heaven one day.

Cindi -
That it's OK to grieve a baby you never saw or held. You lost a grandchild that you were already planning for and dreaming of. Don't think your emotions are unjustified because it could have

been worse if the baby was stillborn or died right after birth. A co-worker, who had lost a young child told me: Everyone has the right to grieve a loss of any kind. Cry for others but don't measure your loss to someone else's loss that seems greater. God didn't call us to bear the burdens of the whole world.

Vicki -
You are not alone in any of this. And, although it is gut wrenching, you will learn to live with the hole(s) in your heart as you navigate this journey. Share your pain and you will find not everyone is afraid and shying away. Those of us who also walk this unwanted path will walk beside you and just be with you. Find a support group and if you can't; start one when you are able. Sharing your story truly helps.

Tracy M. -
Let your children take the lead in how they want to deal with the death. Just be there for support. Show your emotions but don't make it about you. Seek out counseling because you may feel like you're going crazy. I had anxiety attacks for a while. I think most importantly is acknowledging the grandchild after the loss. Say their name to your kids. I got Malory and Brent an ornament for Mya for Christmas. On Mother's and Father's Day I gave them something. On Mya's one year birthday I had Mass said for her at my church and we had a little cake after dinner. I gave them an angel as a present. They want and need to have their baby recognized.

Kathy T. -
Don't be afraid to talk about your loss of your grandchild. Let them know you are a grandparent and call him by his/her given name. Find ways to keep an open dialogue with your kids today, tomorrow, and especially those days that have significance to include your grandbaby's due date, 1st Christmas or birthdays because your grandchild's parents will have heavy hearts wanting their baby to be acknowledged, not forgotten.

Lorrie -

1. Always talk about your deceased grandchild. Say her/his name. Express out loud that you miss them at all family gatherings, especially to your grieving children. Everyone is thinking it. Everyone is already sad about them not being there, so don't worry that you will make anyone cry. Say their name! Cry together! Your grandchild is worth your tears!

2. Always count your deceased grandchild when people ask how many grandchildren you have. That little Being is always and forever your grandchild, and always and forever your child's little baby.

3. Each passing year is different. Your family will never be the family you were before the loss. Healing happens, but it doesn't take you back to where you were before your grandchild died. Some years the anniversaries or birthdays will be easier, some years will be as painful and agonizing as the first. Be flexible and open and kind to yourself and your children... say your grandchild's name, light a candle for them, write their name in the sand at the beach. Above all remember and acknowledge that they were HERE, and they are LOVED.

Allow Yourself Time to Grieve

Grandparents can be so concerned with the pain their children are feeling that they don't allow themselves time to grieve. If you are reading this as a grieving grandparent, know that you have your own grief that will need your attention at some point. Please have someone in your life to go to with your pain. Taking care of you is important so that you can continue to take care of your grieving child.

You, like the child's parents, will walk through your own stages of grief. Most people go through the following common stages of grief: denial, anger, bargaining, depression, and acceptance. Others describe numbness, disorganization, and reorganization. Each individual is unique in their grief experience. A variety of responses are normal and can be expected, such as: anger, resentment, pain, sorrow, bitterness, emptiness, numbness, exhaustion, apathy, depression, and even some joy as you remember your little one, peace as you think of your loved one in heaven. There are so many feelings that come at will and even when the overwhelming sorrow has passed and a new form of normalcy has returned, you may out of nowhere, when you least expect it, feel grief's gripping waves overtake you once more.

If you are in the new stages of grief, overwhelmed with sorrow... wondering if you will feel this way forever... please know this: You are forever changed. But, over time, those changes will become a beautiful part of the tapestry of your life. You will always miss your grandbaby, but you will adjust to a "new normal." You will not feel like you are drowning forever. You will laugh again and take joy in the pleasures of life again... you will. Your life may be different, but it is not without hope.

Be Gentle With Yourself as You Grieve

- Give yourself time and grace to heal. Remember, you are carrying your own grief for your grandchild, and the pain of watching your child grieve the loss of their baby.
- Do things that bring comfort to you. Eat a meal you enjoy, take a warm bath, read a book, watch a movie. Sit on the patio and sip some lemonade.
- Talk with a supportive friend. There's healing for many, in telling their stories.
- Spend some time soaking in nature. Feel the breeze, walk in the grass, listen to the waves lapping against the shore.
- Rest. Grief is physically, emotionally, mentally, and spiritually exhausting. You will need to rest more than normal.
- Exercise and take care of you! Exercise releases natural feel-good endorphins that help us battle depression and the weight of grief. It is also a healthy release for anger and feelings of regret and helplessness.
- Find ways to honor the memory of your grandchild. He or she is worth remembering and celebrating.
- Many grandparents and parents find comfort in helping others or creating something beautiful in memory of their little one. They may also donate to a charity in the baby's name.
- Don't be afraid to reach out to clergy and/or professional counselors for additional support as you process your grief.

- Allow the luxury of a deep belly giggle if you can conjure one to the surface. Soak in moments of joy when they come.
- Thoroughly, unabashedly enjoy your people...your tribe. Whoever they may be.
- Pray a little or read a promise from scripture. And, if you're so broken and done you can't muster words to pray, just sit with Jesus awhile. Just as you are. That's still prayer.

Grieving Grandparents, please know you are not alone. We see you, and the way you quietly carry the pain of grief for your grandchild mixed with the pain of watching your own child grieve for their baby. We see the heavy burden you carry in your heart. While there will always be a missing seat at the table and a missing place in your heart for the baby who was only here for a brief time, the raw grief will not hurt with this intensity forever. Soon, the memories and ache you feel as a family will be woven together in the dance of life... the tears and the joy... woven together.

You began as a dream in my heart, little one.
A someday dream.
A barely whisper.
A promise of hope for the person you
would become.
Tea parties or baseball games.
Party dresses or tuxedos.
We had plans for you, little one.
Dreams for a life not yet lived.
And though your time here was brief,
You were here.
You matter.
You were the dream in my heart.
And, you still are...
Forever in my heart, little one.

~ Kelly Gerken

Helpful Resources

Online Support for Grieving Grandparents
- Walking With You Support Group – available for parents and grandparents grieving the loss of a baby or young child.
- Grieving Grandparents
- The Compassionate Friends
- Grief Share Support Group

There are also a few more Facebook support groups for grandparents if you search.

Books for Grieving Grandparents
- Walking With You for Grieving Grandparents by Kelly Gerken
- Grieving Grandparents by Sherokee Ilse
- A Grandparent's Sorrow by R.N. Pat Schwiebert and Jean Grover
- Healing a Grandparent's Grieving Heart by Alan D. Wolfelt, PhD

Memory-Making and Support
www.sufficientgraceministries.org

Made in the USA
Monee, IL
15 September 2020

42568530R00046